INSIDE THE NFL

NFC EAST

THE DALLAS COWBOYS
THE NEW YORK GIANTS
THE PHILADELPHIA EAGLES
THE WASHINGTON REDSKINS

BY K. C. KELLEY

The Child's World®

Published in the United States of America by
The Child's World® • 1980 Lookout Drive
Mankato, MN 56003-1705
800-599-READ • www.childsworld.com

ACKNOWLEDGEMENTS

The Child's World®: Mary Berendes,
Publishing Director

The Design Lab: Kathleen Petelinsek,
Design; Gregory Lindholm, Page Production

Manuscript consulting and photo research
by Shoreline Publishing Group LLC.

Thanks to Nick Welsh and Jim Gigliotti
for their assistance on this book.

PHOTOS

Front cover: Joe Robbins
Back cover: AP/Wide World
Interior: AP/Wide World: 5, 8, 12, 13, 17, 19, 20,
27, 29; Corbis: 14, 23; Joe Robbins: 6, 11, 24,
26, 30, 32.

LIBRARY OF CONGRESS
CATALOGING-IN-PUBLICATION DATA

Kelley, K. C.
  NFC East / by K.C. Kelley.
    p. cm. — (Inside the NFL)
  Includes bibliographical references and index.
  ISBN 978-1-59296-997-5
(library bound : alk. paper)
  1. National Football League—History—Juvenile
literature. 2. Football—United States—History—
Juvenile literature. I. Title. II. Title: National
Football Conference East. III. Series.
  GV955.5.N35K45 2008
  796.332'640973—dc22   2008010515

INTRODUCTION, 4

CHAPTER ONE
THE DALLAS COWBOYS | 6

CHAPTER TWO
THE NEW YORK GIANTS | 13

CHAPTER THREE
THE PHILADELPHIA EAGLES | 20

CHAPTER FOUR
THE WASHINGTON REDSKINS | 27

TIME LINE, 34
STAT STUFF, 36
GLOSSARY, 39
FIND OUT MORE, 40
INDEX, 40

NFC EAST
INTRODUCTION

When the Dallas Cowboys and the Washington Redskins take the field against each other twice each year, there's hardly a football fan in either of those cities who is not watching. Of course, it's the same thing when the Cowboys play the New York Giants. Or the Giants play the Philadelphia Eagles.

Welcome to the National Football Conference (NFC) East Division, the home of some of **professional** football's greatest **rivalries.** The rivalries in the NFC East are particularly intense because each of these clubs has been around a long time and because they have played together in the same division ever since 1970.

They are also intense because every one of these **franchises** is filled with great tradition, and has featured some championship teams. But don't get the idea that the teams in the NFC East are living off past glory. In 2007, the Giants won the **Super Bowl** for the third time. And three of the four NFC East teams made the **playoffs** that year. The only one that didn't, Philadelphia, still has been one of the league's top teams since the turn of the century.

Read on, and we'll learn more about the teams in this storied division.

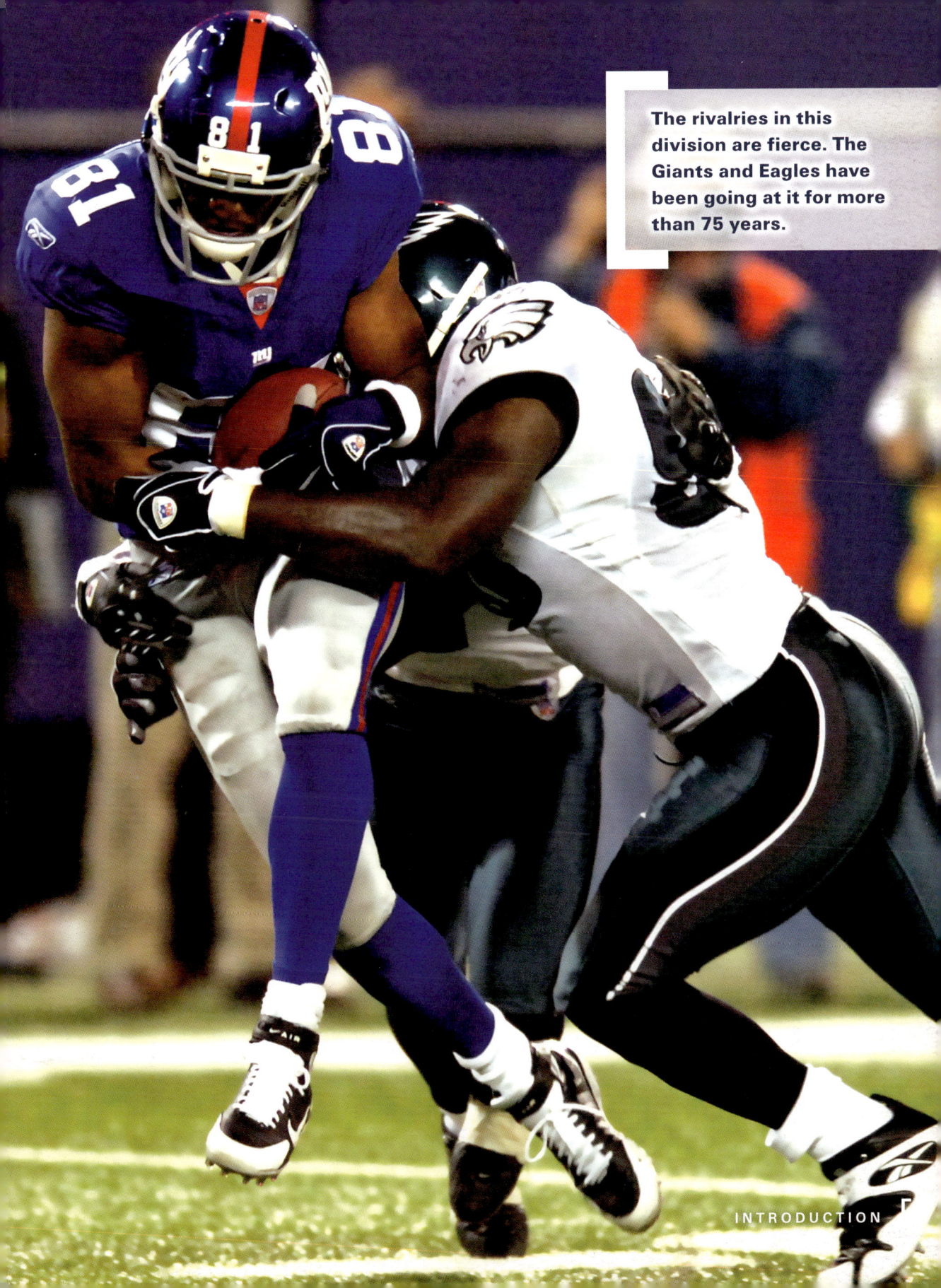

The rivalries in this division are fierce. The Giants and Eagles have been going at it for more than 75 years.

CHAPTER ONE

THE DALLAS COWBOYS

I t's hard to believe that the Dallas Cowboys weren't even part of the NFL for the first 40 seasons of the league's existence. That's because they've crammed more history into their five decades of play since 1960 than even the longest-running NFL franchises.

Along the way, the Cowboys have built such a big and loyal following that they are sometimes called "America's Team." Fans in the United States and all around the world love to cheer on the Cowboys.

For most of the Cowboys' existence, those fans have had lots to cheer about. In fact, Dallas has played in the Super Bowl more times (eight) than any other team. The Cowboys' five wins in the Super Bowl tie the Pittsburgh Steelers and the San Francisco 49ers for the most ever. And even though they haven't been around as long as a lot of other teams, the Cowboys have made it to the playoffs

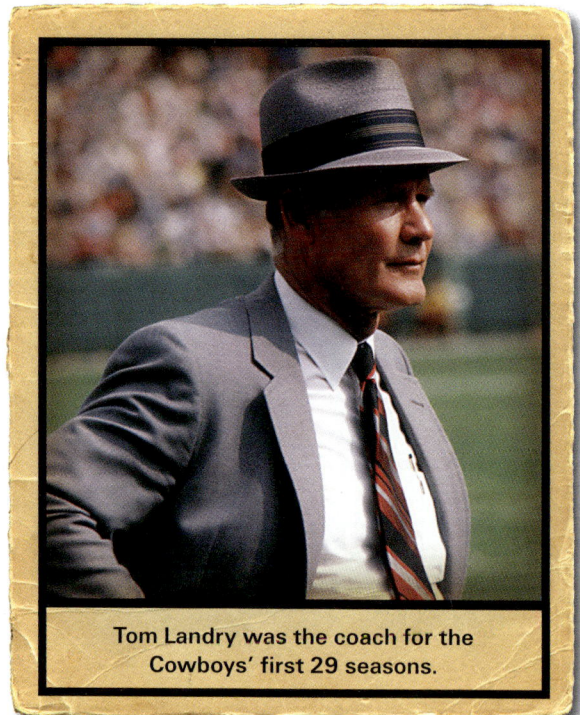

Tom Landry was the coach for the Cowboys' first 29 seasons.

29 times in their history. No other NFL team has been to the **postseason** more often. (The New York Giants, who began play in 1925, also have been in the playoffs 29 times.)

Here's another impressive note: From 1966 to 1985, the Cowboys had a winning record every year. That's an amazing 20 seasons in row. They made the playoffs each year from 1966 to 1973 to set an NFL record of eight **consecutive** postseason appearances. After they missed the playoffs in 1974, they started another string—nine seasons in a row in the playoffs through 1983 to break their own record!

No one could have guessed the Cowboys would have such great success watching them in their first season in 1960, though. They lost their first 10 games, and the best they could do was one tie game that year. They didn't win their first game until their second season. And it wasn't until their sixth season in business that the Cowboys managed even to win as many games as they lost.

But the Cowboys' original owner, Clint Murchison Jr., and general manager, Tex Schramm, were very patient. Even as they suffered one losing season after another, they knew they had the key ingredients to build a winning team. The only thing they needed was time. So they stuck with Tom Landry, the man they hired as their first coach in 1960.

Landry had been the defensive genius behind the New York Giants' great teams of the 1950s. Schramm and Murchison were so impressed by

How does the "Dallas Rangers" sound? That was the original name when the franchise was officially awarded in January of 1960. By March of that year, however, the club decided to go with "Dallas Cowboys" instead.

Landry's football smarts that they signed him for an extra 10 years after his third straight losing season. Gil Brandt was in charge of choosing players. He brought a modern and scientific approach to scouting college players. The first player he ever got through the NFL **draft** was defensive tackle Bob Lilly, who enjoyed a superb career and was later inducted into the Pro Football Hall of Fame. Lilly, who played from 1961 to 1974, remains such a big part of the team's history that he is known to Dallas fans as "Mr. Cowboy."

Schramm himself knew football inside and out. Even more, he understood the importance of television and marketing, unlike most owners or executives of the time. Among his many ideas was using television instant replay as an officiating tool.

The Cowboys have always had great players. But rather than build teams around great players, the Cowboys built their success around a great system. Brandt and Landry had a knack for knowing what players to plug into that system and where. Much sooner than other teams, the Cowboys devised a wide variety of offensive and defensive formations. Just before the ball was snapped, they would shift into another formation to confuse other teams.

On offense, their quarterbacks sometimes lined up a few yards behind the center instead of directly over the center. This "Shotgun" formation gives the quarterback a little more time to look downfield for receivers. The Cowboys didn't invent the Shotgun, but they did show how it could be

Quarterback Roger Staubach was so good, he had more than one nickname! He was known as "Roger the Dodger" for his ability to elude defenders. He was also called "Captain Comeback" for often bringing the Cowboys from behind to win.

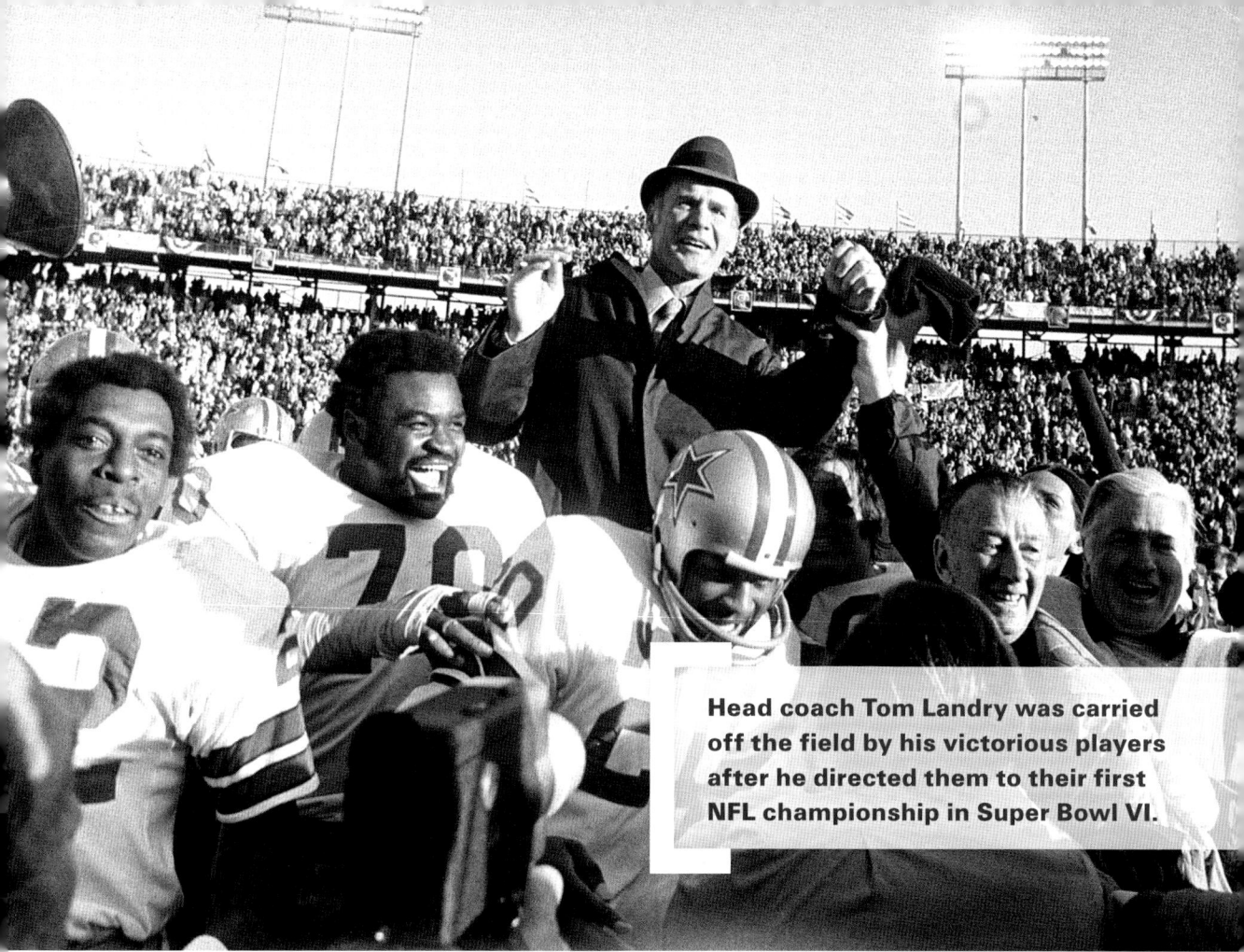

Head coach Tom Landry was carried off the field by his victorious players after he directed them to their first NFL championship in Super Bowl VI.

used effectively in a modern offense. In the 1970s, quarterback Roger Staubach combined this strategy with his famous **scrambling** skills to lead Dallas to new heights.

When it came to the Cowboys' defense, size was important. They often drafted very large players —such as Ed "Too Tall" Jones—to stop the run and attack quarterbacks. Under Landry's strict control, the team evolved into an efficient winning machine. He had no patience for players who wouldn't submit to his system. Those players, no matter how talented, quickly found themselves traded to other teams.

The Cowboys' patience paid off in the 1971 season when Dallas won Super Bowl VI, its first league championship. Throughout the 1970s, they remained among the league's best teams. They played in

Troy Aikman never had eye-popping statistics, but he was a great leader. Aikman quarterbacked Dallas to three Super Bowl wins in the 1990s.

three other Super Bowls that decade, winning Super Bowl XII. The team had some down years in the 1980s until a new owner came into town and cleaned house.

The Cowboys were sold to Jerry Jones in 1989. Legendary coach Landry was fired. Landry's replacement, Jimmy Johnson, suffered two losing years, but he assembled a great **core** of players. Quarterback Troy Aikman, receiver Michael Irvin, and running back Emmitt Smith were called the "Triplets." They made up one of the NFL's best offensive trios.

The Cowboys are scheduled to move into a new stadium in Arlington, Texas, in 2009. The stadium will have a **retractable** roof. Since 1971, the team has played in Texas Stadium in Irving. It has a hole in the roof that covers the fans but leaves the field open to the elements. Linebacker D.D. Lewis once said the hole in the roof was "so God can watch his favorite team."

Aikman was a strong-armed passer with great leadership skills. Irvin combined speed and size to score dozens of touchdowns. Along with Smith, they helped Dallas return to the top of the NFL. The team won three Super Bowls in four seasons, from 1992 to 1995.

Smith was the soul of the great Cowboys teams of the 1990s. He led the NFL in rushing four times and set a team record with 1,713 yards in 1992. In 1995, he broke his own record by rushing a total of 1,773 yards. Though smaller than some runners, he was a determined, powerful player. On his way to becoming the NFL's all-time leading rusher in 2002, Smith made millions of fans.

By 2003, Smith had left the club, but there was a new sheriff in town: head coach Bill Parcells, who was hired after Dallas suffered a string of poor seasons. Parcells, who previously had led the Giants, Patriots, and Jets to the playoffs, made an immediate impact. In his first season, he doubled the Cowboys' win total from 5 the previous year (in 2002) to 10 and had Dallas back in the playoffs.

Although Parcells was not able to bring Dallas back to the Super Bowl in his four seasons from 2003 to 2006, he did find a new star in quarterback Tony Romo and brought in an established star in wide receiver Terrell Owens.

Romo, an undrafted player out of college in 2003, spent his first three seasons with the Cowboys learning under Parcells. Then, in 2006, an injury to starting quarterback Drew Bledsoe

Behind big-play wide receiver Terrell Owens (81) and quarterback Tony Romo (9), the Cowboys have remained among the NFL's best teams.

put Romo in the lineup. Owens, who is very talented but has clashed with coaches and teammates in the past, signed as a free agent in '06 and caught 13 touchdown passes his first year in Dallas. Together, Romo and Owens led the team to the playoffs.

Parcells resigned the next year, but Romo and Owens were even better for new coach Wade Phillips. Romo passed for 4,211 yards and 36 touchdowns, Owens caught 15 scoring passes, and Dallas tied a franchise record by winning 13 games.

The Cowboys were upset by the division-rival Giants in the playoffs that year. Still, they showed that "America's Team" may be headed to America's biggest game—the Super Bowl—again soon.

CHAPTER TWO

THE NEW YORK GIANTS

I n the early days of the NFL, the league knew that it had to succeed in New York, America's largest and most important city, if it was going to succeed nationally. So in 1925, the Giants were born. The new club soon was a hit, both on the field and at the gate. And it's been that way pretty much ever since. The Giants have won seven NFL championships—including a magical run to Super Bowl XLII in the 2007 season—and played in the league title game many other times. And it's tough to get a ticket at Giants Stadium, which **annually** is sold out.

That's a long way from the 1920s, when the American public wasn't sure about the NFL just yet. The league was made up mostly of teams in Ohio, Illinois, and Wisconsin, so the league approached Tim Mara and offered him a

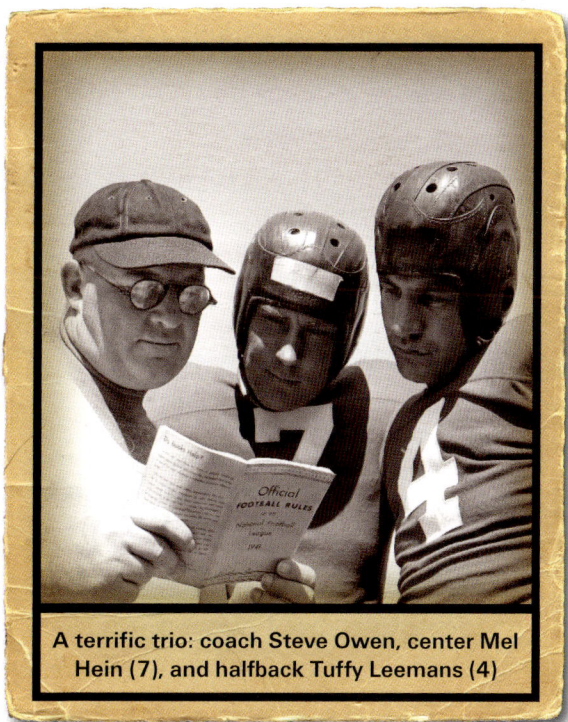

A terrific trio: coach Steve Owen, center Mel Hein (7), and halfback Tuffy Leemans (4)

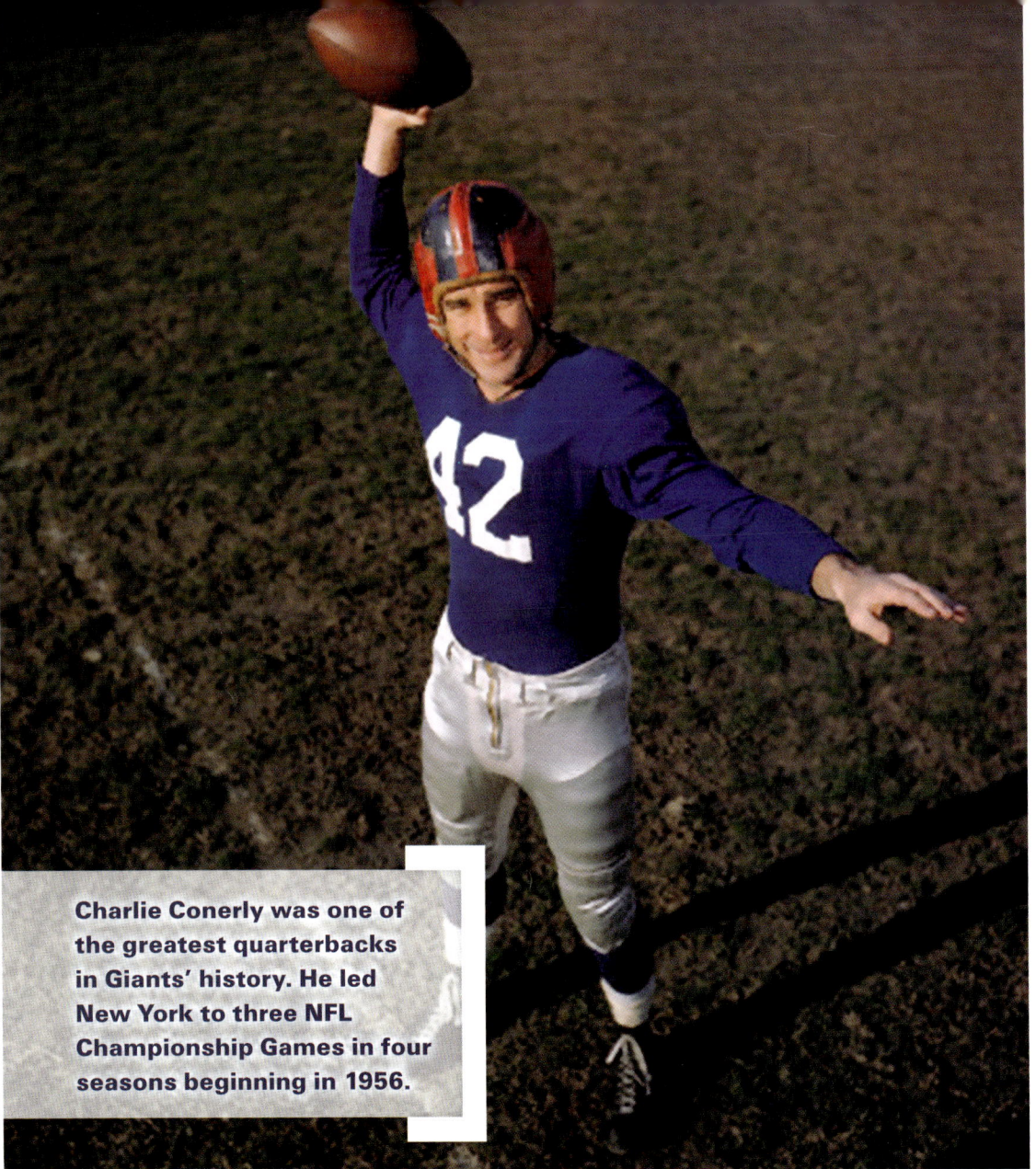

Charlie Conerly was one of the greatest quarterbacks in Giants' history. He led New York to three NFL Championship Games in four seasons beginning in 1956.

franchise in New York for $500. "I figured a franchise for anything in New York was worth $500," Mara said. The team is worth more than $300 million today, so you might say that was a good investment.

Mara's team played in the Polo Grounds. He named the club after New York's baseball team, which also played there. But not enough people showed up to watch the Giants play at first. Within months, Mara had lost $40,000 on his new franchise. He might have gone out of business. And if the NFL didn't make it in New York, who knows what would have happened to the league?

In November of 1925, however, the Chicago Bears signed halfback Red Grange, who had been an enormously popular player in college at Illinois. Grange and the Bears visited New York for a game early in December. The Giants lost 19–7, but the big story was the crowd. More than 73,000 fans—a pro record at the time—jammed the Polo Grounds. That turned the Giants' finances around. The franchise not only survived, but it **thrived.**

Two years later, in 1927, the Giants won their first championship. They won more games that season (11) than any other team and held opponents to a season total of only 20 points. Other titles soon followed in 1934 and 1938, then another in 1956. The Giants also have won championships in 1986 (Super Bowl XXI), 1990 (XXV), and 2007 (XLII).

In 1931, the Giants hired Steve Owen as coach. Owen had been a stellar tackle for the Giants, and he would end up being coach for 23 years. Under Owen, the Giants played in the very first NFL Championship Game against the Chicago Bears in 1933. However, the Bears beat the Giants 23–21 in a classic nail-biter in which the lead changed hands six times.

The next year, 1934, the Giants made it to the championship, again facing the Bears. The temperature was 9 degrees (minus-13 C), and the ground was hard as ice. The players were slipping and sliding around in their cleats. At halftime, the Giants' trainer gave his players "basketball shoes"— sneakers. This gave the Giants a huge advantage over the Bears. The New York players had much better footing on the icy field. They scored four touchdowns in the second half to win. The contest is still remembered as "The Sneakers Game."

Under Owen, the Giants remained contenders until the end of World War II. Owen was replaced in 1954 by Jim Lee Howell, an ex-Marine and also a former Giant. In the eight seasons from 1956 to 1963, the Giants finished in first place six times. They won the NFL championship in 1956 and played in the championship games of 1958 and 1959, losing both of those games to the Baltimore Colts. (The 1958 game is still called "The Greatest Game Ever Played." Giants fans might not think so, but the Colts' thrilling **overtime** win remains a classic.)

The Giants had an abundance of talent: quarterbacks Charlie Conerly and Y. A. Tittle, running back Frank Gifford, linebacker Sam Huff, and defensive back Emlen Tunnell, to name just a few. Two assistant coaches, Vince Lombardi and Tom Landry, later became legendary head coaches.

However, after 1963, the Giants experienced a 20-year downhill slide. They would play in four different "home" stadiums. They finally moved into Giants Stadium in New Jersey in 1976. However, they finished last or next-to-last eight times between 1976 and 1987.

The 1986 Giants popularized the tradition of dousing their head coach with ice water or a sports drink after a big victory. Lots of teams do that now.

Linebacker Lawrence Taylor (56) was one of the greatest defensive players ever. He starred for the Giants from 1981 to 1993.

But in the 1980s, under coach Bill Parcells, the Giants transformed themselves. They turned from the 98-pound weakling of the league to the 900-pound gorilla. Offensively, the Giants' game plan was simple, basic, and aggressive. They focused heavily on running the ball. On defense, they were fierce. Lawrence Taylor may have been the best linebacker ever. Other teams often double-teamed Taylor (or triple-teamed him!), which freed up his teammates to make the play. But Taylor still was the most dominant player. Taylor and Parcells led the Giants to victories in Super Bowls XXI and XXV.

The Giants have returned to the Super Bowl two more times since. In 2000, Giants coach Jim Fassel stunned the **media** when he said late in the year that the team wouldn't lose any more games during the regular season. Amazingly, the Giants did what their coach said. They won their last five games and then beat Philadelphia and Minnesota to earn a trip to Super Bowl XXXV. But the Ravens' defense was too much in a 34–7 rout.

Still, Giants' fans got to watch two of the greatest players in club history in the 2000s. On offense, running back Tiki Barber became the club's all-time leading rusher. On defense, end Michael Strahan became one of the top quarterback sackers in league history.

By 2007, Barber had retired but Strahan was still a force. Quarterback Eli Manning, the younger brother of the Colts' Peyton Manning, emerged as a leader. He sparked another late-season surge that carried the Giants to the Super Bowl. This time, New York stunned undefeated New England with a 17–14 victory that ranks as one of the greatest upsets in NFL history. The winning points came on Eli Manning's touchdown pass to Plaxico Burress with only 35 seconds left.

In 1930, Tim Mara handed the team over to his two sons, Jack and Wellington. At the time, Wellington was only 14 years old. Wellington was seen regularly at practices and games until his death in 2005.

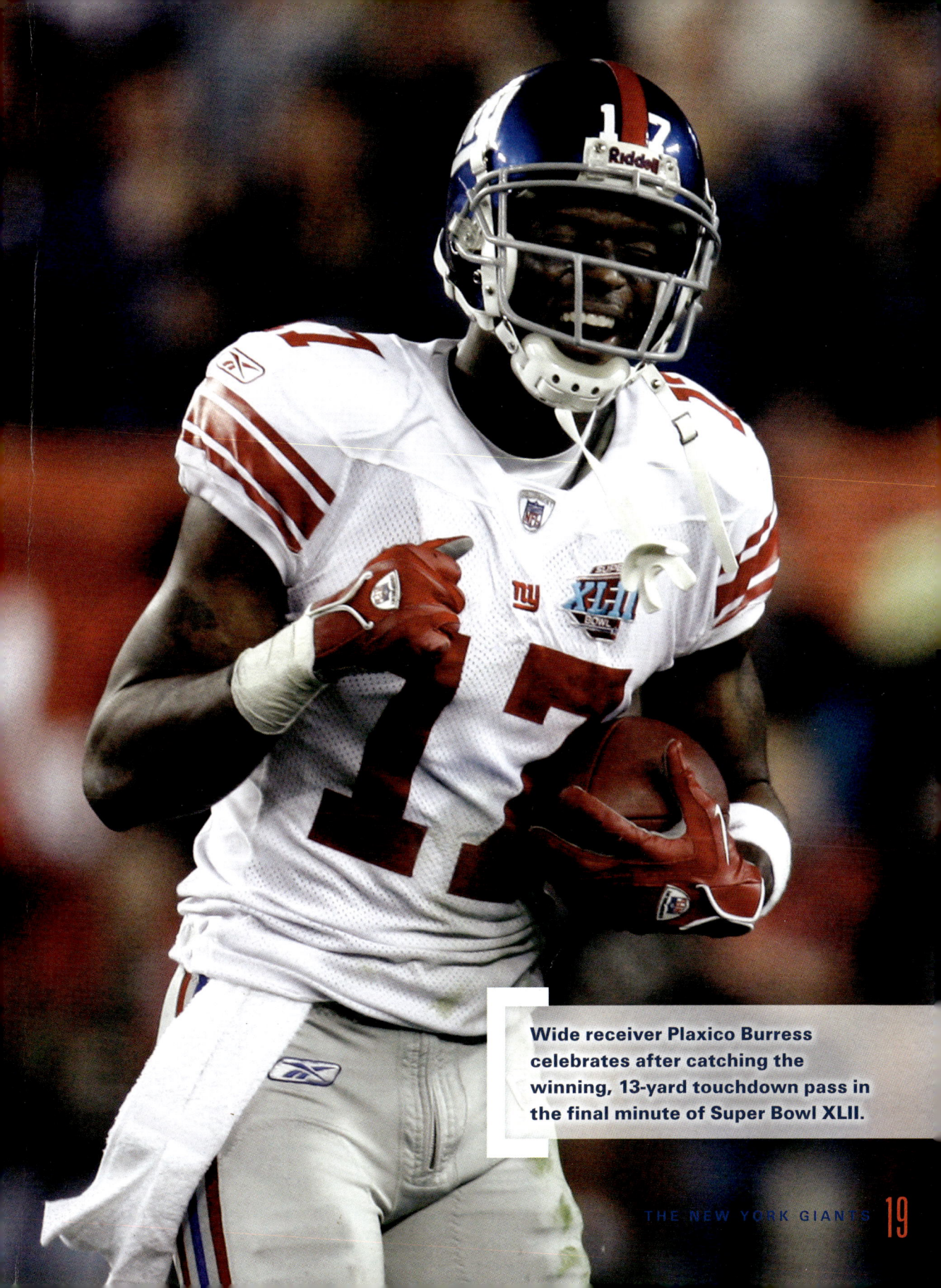

Wide receiver Plaxico Burress celebrates after catching the winning, 13-yard touchdown pass in the final minute of Super Bowl XLII.

CHAPTER THREE

THE PHILADELPHIA EAGLES

With head coach Andy Reid and quarterback Donovan McNabb leading the way, the Philadelphia Eagles have been one of the NFL's most **consistent** winners of the 2000s. They reached the playoffs six times in the first seven seasons of the decade, and they played in four consecutive conference championship games beginning in 2001. That streak was capped by a Super Bowl appearance in the 2004 season.

It hasn't always been that way in Philadelphia, though. In fact, the Eagles got off to a very slow start after they were founded in 1933. They lost their opening game, 56–0. In 1936, they lost 11 straight games, including six in which they didn't even score. They didn't post a winning season in their first 10 years, and they usually hovered near last place in the standings.

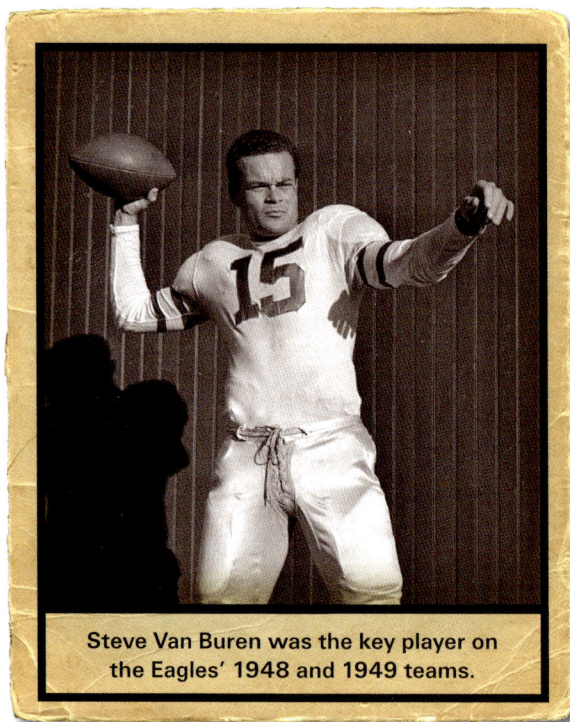

Steve Van Buren was the key player on the Eagles' 1948 and 1949 teams.

One good thing came out of those struggles, though. Owner Bert Bell (the future NFL **commissioner**) was concerned that teams such as the Chicago Bears and New York Giants were getting all the best players coming out of college, and that the other teams in the league wouldn't be able to compete. So in 1935, he proposed a draft of college players, with the teams with the poorest records picking first. Bell's proposal was **ratified,** and the NFL held its first draft in 1936.

In the mid-1940s, the Eagles turned the corner. In 1944, they drafted future Pro Football Hall of Fame running back Steve Van Buren in the first round. Philadelphia soon combined the hard-charging running of Van Buren with the pass catching of end Pete Pihos. Add in a fearsome defense and the coaching of Earle "Greasy" Neale, and the Eagles had a pretty tough team.

In 1947, the Eagles tied for the Eastern Division championship, and then shut out Pittsburgh 21–0 in a playoff game. The Chicago Cardinals ended Philadelphia's championship hopes in the title game, but that was only a temporary setback.

In 1948 and 1949, the Eagles won the NFL title. In both championship games, they shut out their opponents (the Chicago Cardinals, 7–0, and the Los Angeles Rams, 14–0). No other team since has done that.

In the 1948 championship game, a blinding snowstorm made the field nearly invisible. Players huddled under straw blankets on the sidelines.

Amid the tough conditions, the Eagles' defense limited the Cardinals to just six first downs. Van Buren scored the game's only points on a 5-yard touchdown run. Bad weather dominated the following year's championship, too. Heavy rains transformed the field into a muddy river. However, Van Buren splashed through the puddles to run for a then-record 196 yards.

That 1949 team included Chuck Bednarik, one of the toughest and most punishing players ever to lace up football cleats. As a linebacker and center, he was one of the last players to play both offense and defense. "Concrete Charley" played in 253 out of a possible 256 games during his 14-year career. During the 1960 championship game, in which Philadelphia beat Green Bay 17–13, Bednarik played all but two of the 60 minutes. On the last play of the game, he saved the win by stopping Packers fullback Jim Taylor from scoring. Leading the Eagles' offense in that game was Hall of Fame quarterback Norm Van Brocklin.

After winning the 1960 championship—and coming close the next year—the Eagles slid steadily downhill for nearly 20 years. By the early 1970s, the Eagles were not just losing, but also fighting among themselves. One coach called the team's owner "a man of little character," and was fired. After he was fired, his replacement—who believed in a military-style of team discipline—ordered all players to cut their hair short and shave their beards and mustaches. None of this produced a winning season.

The Eagles didn't have their own team in 1943. Because of manpower shortages during World War II, they combined with the Pittsburgh Steelers to form what was unofficially called the "Steagles" team. Officially, the team was called "Phil-Pitt."

Rifle-armed quarterback Ron Jaworski helped carry the Eagles to the Super Bowl for the first time in 1980.

Things changed for the better in 1976 when the Eagles hired Dick Vermeil as head coach. Strict, hard-working, and emotional, Vermeil pushed his players to new levels. Quarterback Ron Jaworski was smart, sturdy, and dependable. Wide receiver Harold Carmichael was 6 feet 8 inches (203 centimeters) tall, and still holds the Eagles' record for receptions. Ferocious linebacker Bill Bergey led the defense.

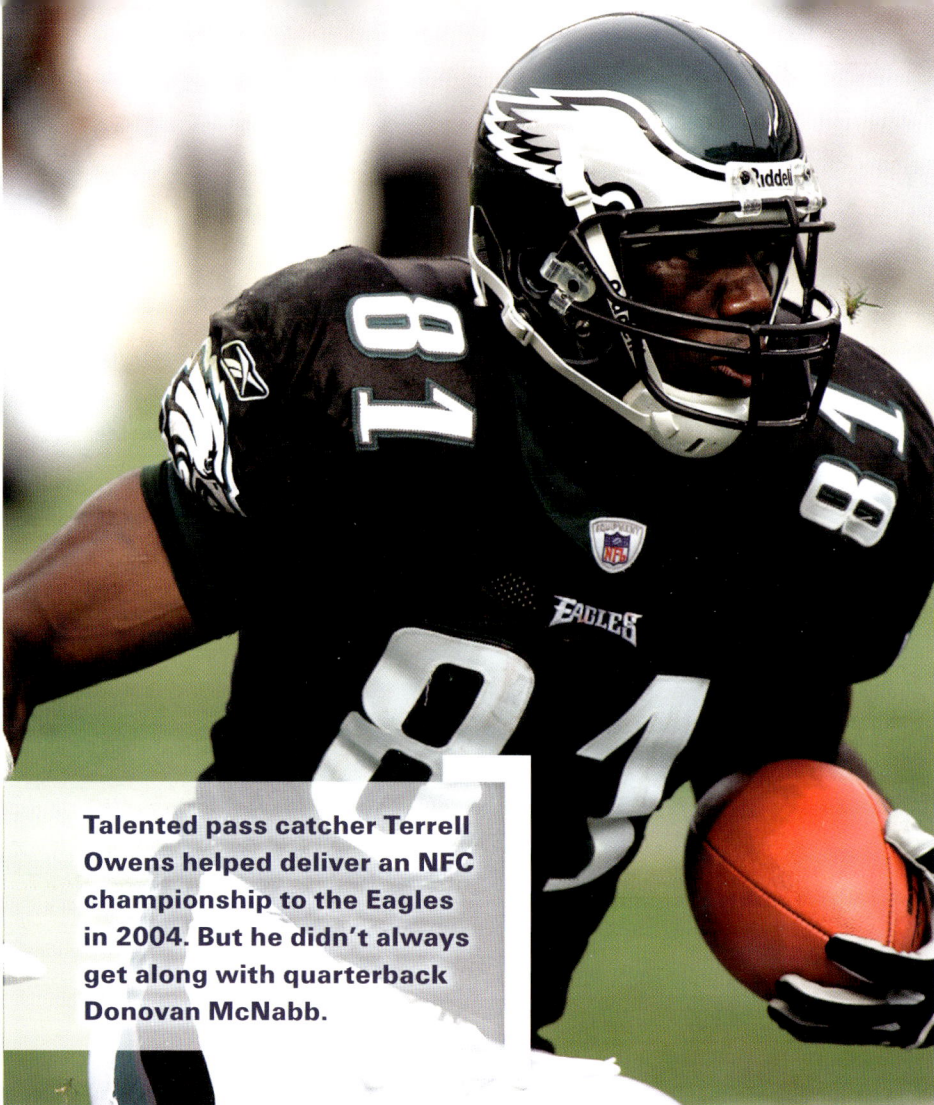

Talented pass catcher Terrell Owens helped deliver an NFC championship to the Eagles in 2004. But he didn't always get along with quarterback Donovan McNabb.

Running back Wilbert Montgomery became the team's all-time leader in rushing yards. The revamped Eagles made it to the playoffs four years in a row from 1978 to 1981. In 1980, they reached Super Bowl XV, losing to the Oakland Raiders.

Defensive genius Buddy Ryan took over as coach in 1986. With the Eagles, Ryan created a defensive machine that scared opponents before they stepped foot on the field. Defensive linemen Reggie White and Jerome Brown shut down opponents' running games and ate quarterbacks for lunch. Quarterback Randall Cunningham was a gifted long passer and a great scrambler, but he was inconsistent.

The Eagles made the playoffs four times between 1988 and 1992, but never advanced past the divisional round.

Current coach Andy Reid has rallied the Eagles back to winning form. Quarterback Donovan McNabb is 6 feet, 2 inches (188 cm), 226 pounds (103 kg), and as big, fast, and strong as many of the players trying to tackle him. And the Eagles' defense still gives ground—and allows points—as grudgingly as ever.

Together, Reid, McNabb, and the defense helped carry the Eagles to three consecutive NFC Championship Games beginning in 2001, but Philadelphia lost each time. Then, in 2004, the Eagles traded for the man they believed was the last piece to the Super Bowl puzzle: game-breaking wide receiver Terrell Owens.

Owens was an immediate hit, catching 3 touchdown passes in his first game for Philadelphia and going on to set a new club record with 14 scoring receptions for the season. The Eagles made it to their fourth conference title game in a row and this time, despite an injury to Owens, they beat Atlanta to reach the Super Bowl for the first time in 24 years.

With Owens back in the lineup, Philadelphia gave defending-champion New England all it could handle in Super Bowl XXXIX. Ultimately, though, the Patriots prevailed 24–21.

Owens clashed with McNabb and lasted only one more season in Philadelphia, but the Eagles returned to the top of the NFC East in 2006. They

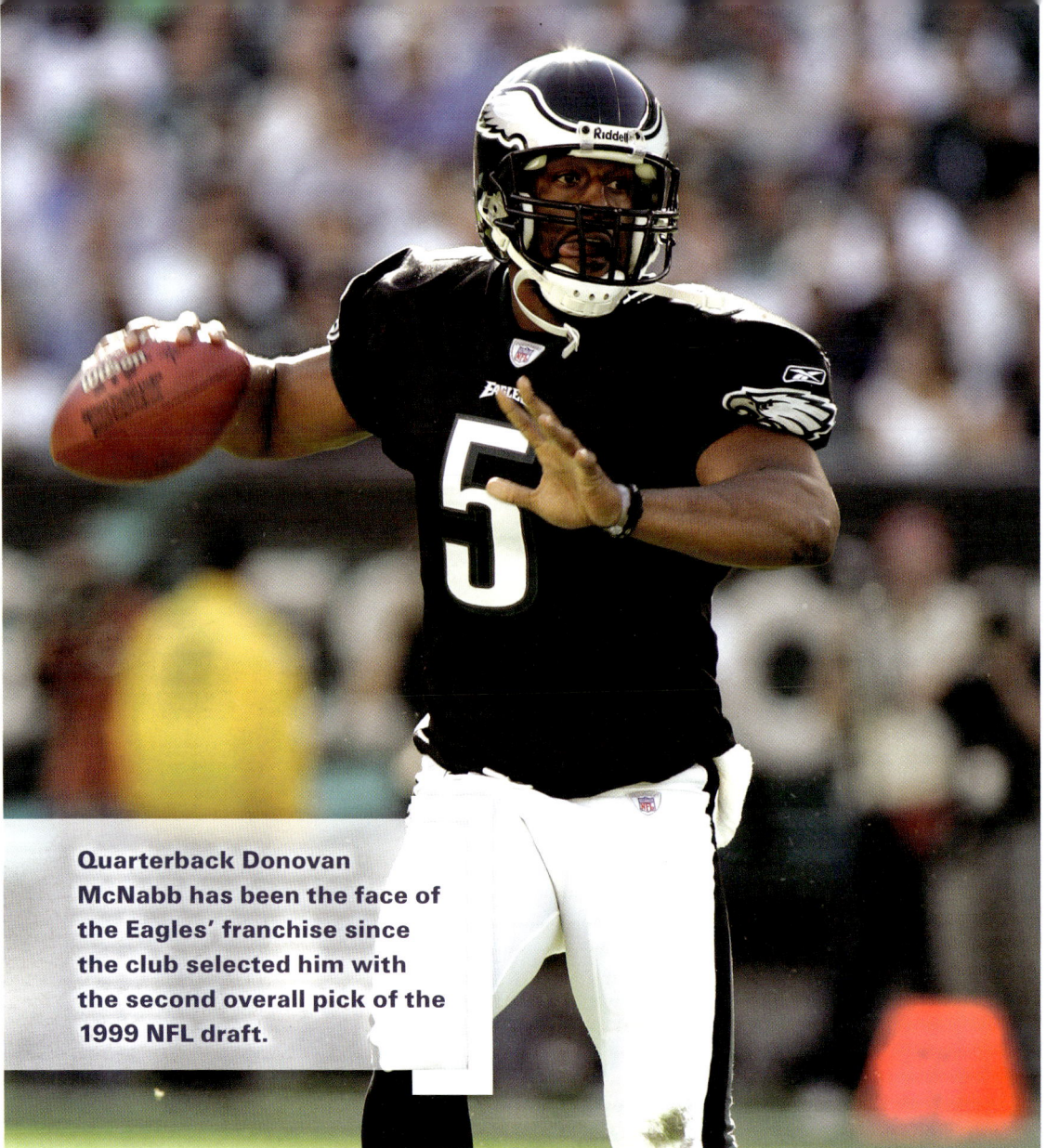

Quarterback Donovan McNabb has been the face of the Eagles' franchise since the club selected him with the second overall pick of the 1999 NFL draft.

beat the division-rival Giants in the opening round of the playoffs, but had their Super Bowl hopes denied by a three-point loss to New Orleans in a divisional playoff game.

It was another heartbreak for Eagles fans, who are still waiting for their first NFL title since 1960. But with Reid at the helm, McNabb at quarterback, and players such as versatile Pro Bowl star Brian Westbrook at running back, those fans hope their team is ready to make another run at the Super Bowl.

THE WASHINGTON REDSKINS

The Washington Redskins may have been the first NFL team to view a football game as a complete entertainment experience for the fans. George Preston Marshall, who founded the club in the 1930s, was a showman, and his wife was a silent-film star. The **flamboyant** Marshall formed the NFL's first marching band, and he and his wife penned a team fight song. Marshall introduced big halftime shows and sideline cheerleaders.

Whatever Marshall did, it worked. The Redskins built one of the NFL's biggest followings. Today, they routinely sell out the largest stadium in the league: 91,704-seat FedExField. Of course, winning is what entertains fans the most, and the Redskins have done plenty of that, too. They have won five NFL championships in all, including three Super Bowls under head coach Joe Gibbs in the 1980s and 1990s. Their first championship came in 1937, in their first season in Washington.

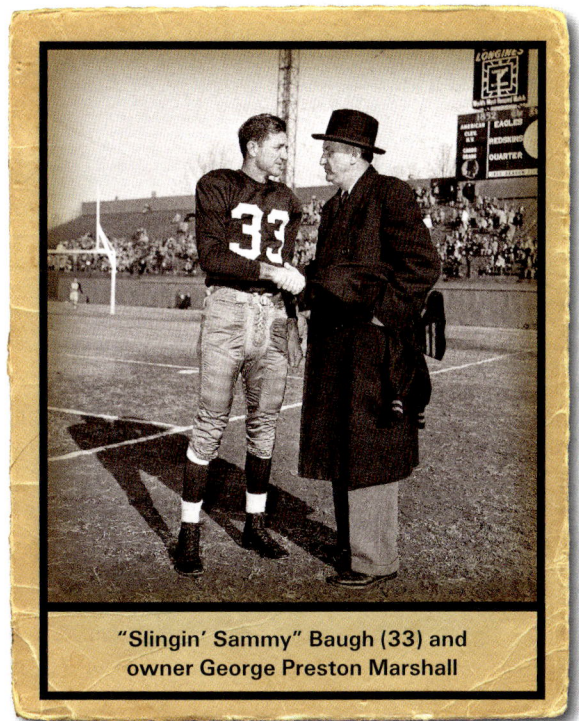

"Slingin' Sammy" Baugh (33) and owner George Preston Marshall

Before that, the Redskins were based in Boston. Marshall, who had built a successful laundry business in Washington, D.C., joined an NFL ownership group in Boston in 1932. He soon became sole owner because his partners dropped out. Marshall and his original partners named the team the Braves because they played on the same field as the Boston Braves baseball team.

After Marshall became sole owner, though, he changed the name to Redskins in 1933. Playing off the team's new name, he had his players show up for team photographs dressed in war paint and war bonnets. He even hired a Native American, William "Lone Star" Dietz, to coach the team.

At the time, no one objected to the team's new name. These days, many Native Americans do object to the name. They feel that the word is a racist slur. However, the team says that its name honors the brave and powerful Native American warriors. At present, the team has no plans to change the name.

The early Boston teams starred running back Cliff Battles. He was the first player ever to rush for more than 200 yards in a game. After several seasons that weren't very good, the Braves won the NFL's Eastern Division in 1936 and advanced to the league championship game. But Marshall didn't feel the team was getting enough support in Boston. So he moved the title game to the Polo Grounds in New York. Green Bay won the game, and the Redskins packed up and headed to their new home in Washington for the 1937 season.

The game to decide the 1937 Eastern Division championship was in New York between the Redskins and the Giants. Some 10,000 Washington fans made the trip, and owner George Preston Marshall—always the showman—marched them up Broadway behind the Redskins' band! (Washington won the game, 49–14.)

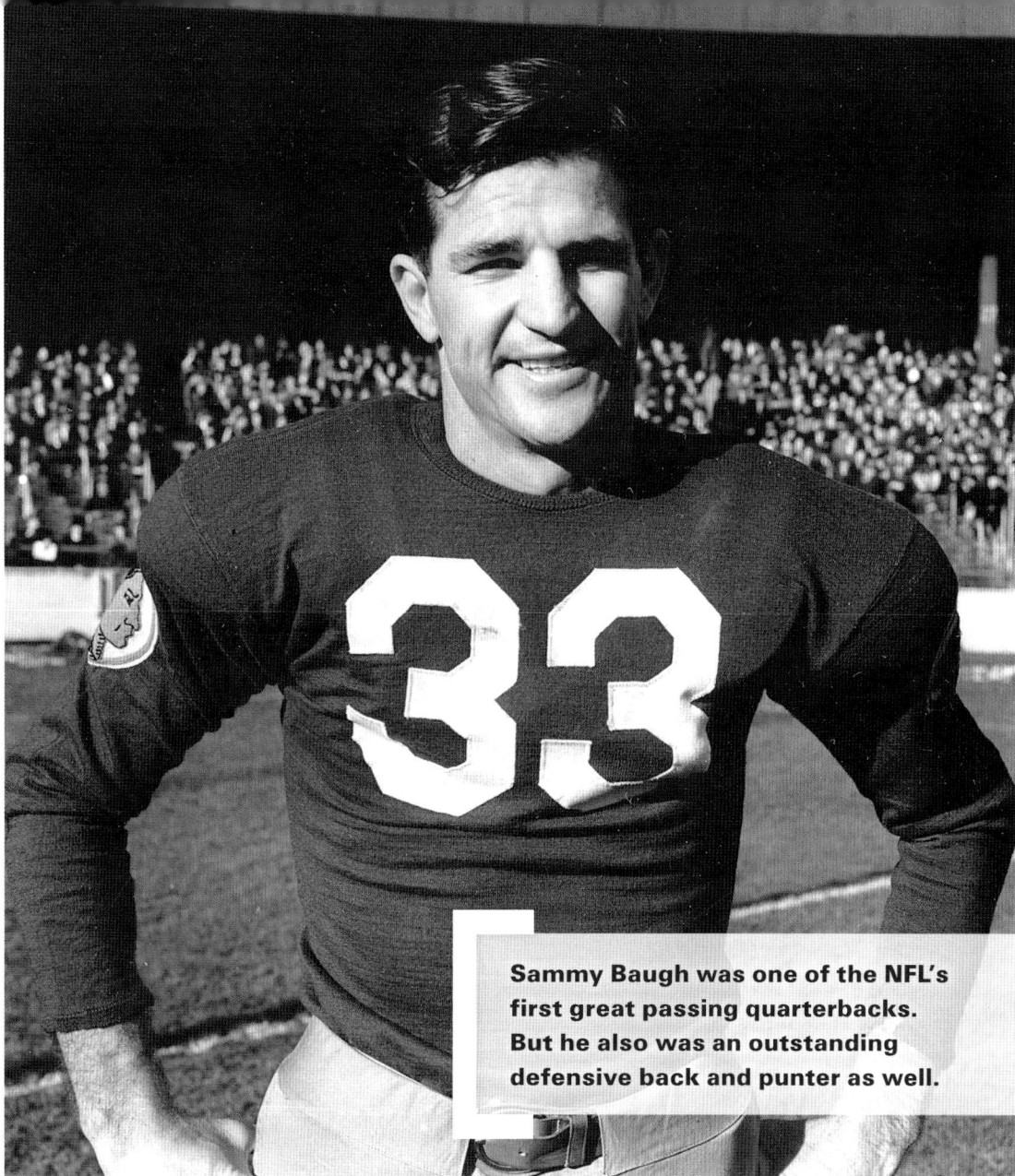

Sammy Baugh was one of the NFL's first great passing quarterbacks. But he also was an outstanding defensive back and punter as well.

The Redskins rewarded their new fans with their first NFL championship. Washington finished 8–3 to win the Eastern Division again, and then upset the Bears 28–21 in Chicago to win the title.

That Washington club was led by **rookie** "Slingin' Sammy" Baugh. During his 16-year career, Baugh—a tough, raw-boned quarterback out of Texas—set dozens of records. At that time, players

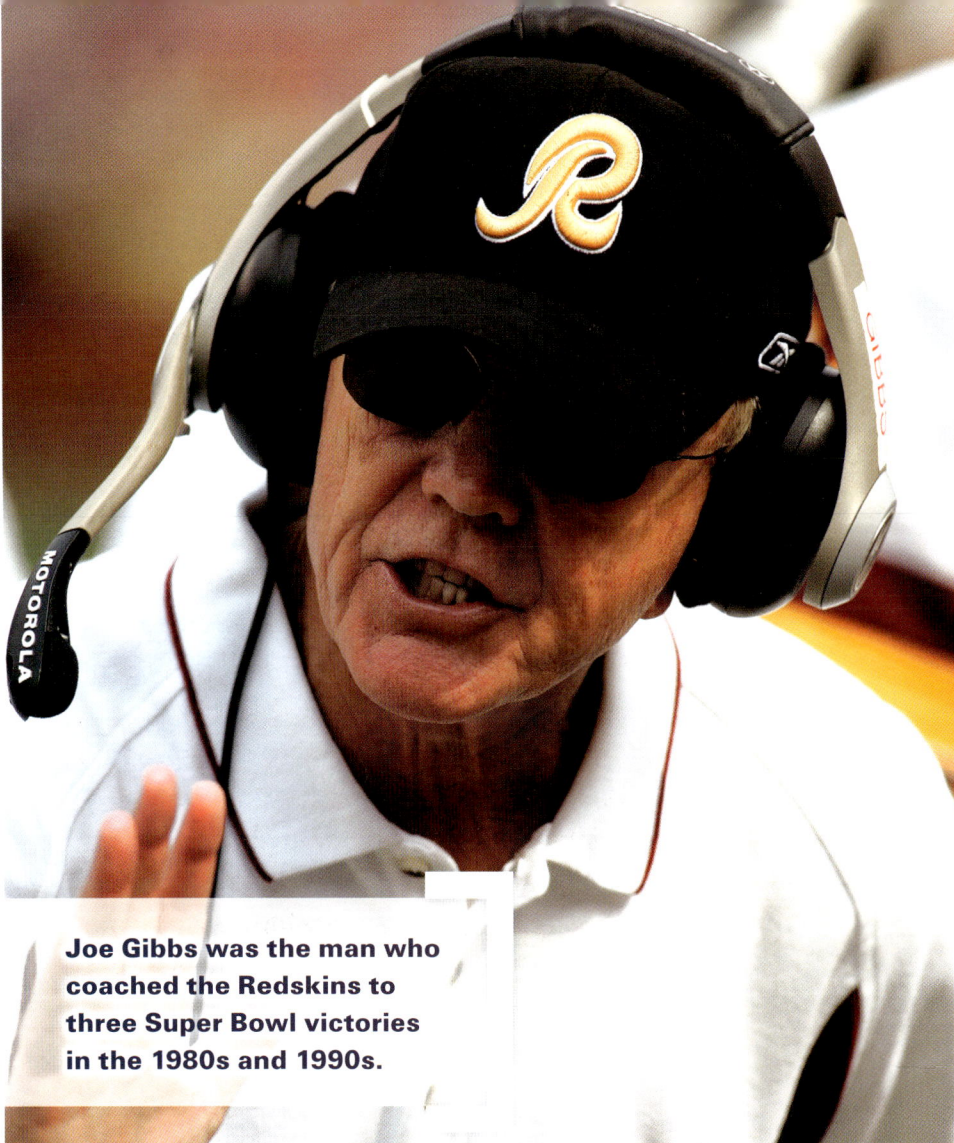

Joe Gibbs was the man who coached the Redskins to three Super Bowl victories in the 1980s and 1990s.

were expected to play both offense and defense. In a 1943 game against the Detroit Lions, Baugh threw four touchdown passes and also intercepted four passes. That year, he led the league in punting, passing, and interceptions—an accomplishment that will never be equaled. His career average of 45.1 yards per punt remained an NFL record for more than 50 years. In 1963, Baugh joined Marshall and 15 others as the original inductees into the Pro Football Hall of Fame.

Baugh also quarterbacked the Redskins' 1942 squad. That year, Washington was a heavy underdog against the Chicago

Bears, who had not lost a game all season, in the NFL Championship Game. But the Redskins remembered a 73–0 drubbing at the hands of the Bears in the 1940 title game. Washington got its revenge with a 14–6 upset.

The Redskins had three more good seasons after that, but between 1946 and 1969, they ranked as one of the worst teams in football. In that time, they won more than half their games in only three seasons. Part of the problem was that Marshall had been reluctant to hire African-American players. When Bobby Mitchell, the team's first African-American player, joined the Redskins in 1962, it helped the team improve.

In 1964, Washington acquired quarterback Sonny Jurgensen, one of the greatest pure passers of all time. Jurgensen teamed with Mitchell and wide receiver Charley Taylor to lead the Redskins to some good seasons.

In 1971, Coach George Allen took over and began to rally the team. In his rush to victory, Allen traded away many talented young players for seasoned veterans. His teams were known as the "Over-the-Hill Gang." Allen's squad made it to Super Bowl VII in 1972, and he never had a losing season as a head coach.

Beginning in 1981, with the hiring of Joe Gibbs as coach, the Redskins achieved their greatest glory. During Gibbs' first 12-year stint with the team, the Redskins went to the Super Bowl four times and won three. The real stars of Gibbs' teams were not flashy quarterbacks but

Running back Clinton Portis has shouldered the load for the Redskins' offense in recent years. He gained 1,262 yards on the ground in 2007.

sturdy offensive linemen who were nicknamed the "Hogs." The Hogs ripped open huge holes for punishing running backs such as John Riggins. The Hogs were so popular that a group of Redskins fans started showing up to games dressed as "Hogettes." They wore women's clothes and had plastic pig snouts strapped to their faces.

Since then, the Redskins' fortunes have been up and down. In 1997, they moved from their previous home in RFK Stadium to their present location at FedExField. A big change came in 1999, when young Daniel Snyder bought the team. He spent a lot of money and made a lot of headlines, but has not turned his team back into a Super Bowl winner yet.

Not even a big-name coach, Steve Spurrier, had any luck. Spurrier, a former NFL player who built a dazzling reputation as an offensive-minded coach in college, managed to win only 12 games in two seasons (seven wins in 2002 and five in 2003) before Snyder went back to the future: He re-hired Gibbs to coach the team in 2004.

Gibbs immediately turned to an old formula to try to return the Redskins to prominence. He traded for workhorse running back Clinton Portis, who gained 1,315 yards in his first season in Washington and 1,516 yards the next. Gibbs lasted four seasons his second time around as coach and took the team to the playoffs twice. But he stepped down after a loss in the wild-card round in 2007. Former Seattle Seahawks quarterback Jim Zorn became the new coach for 2008.

TIME LINE

1932
Washington Redskins are founded as Boston Braves

1933
Philadelphia Eagles are founded; Boston Braves change their name to Boston Redskins

1956
Giants win their first NFL title in 18 years

1925
New York Giants founded; they join the five-year-old NFL

1934
Giants win their first NFL championship

1920 **1930** **1940** **1950** **1960**

1937
Redskins move to Washington and win their first NFL championship

1960
Dallas Cowboys join the NFL as an expansion team; Eagles win league championship

1938
Giants win the league title for the second time in five years

1948
Eagles win the first of back-to-back NFL championships

1942
Redskins stun unbeaten Bears to win the league title

2007
Giants win the NFC title before shocking the Patriots in Super Bowl XLII

2004
Eagles win the NFC championship (their first since 1980), but lose to the New England Patriots in Super Bowl XXXIX

1977
Dallas wins Super Bowl XII

1971
Cowboys win Super Bowl VI for their first NFL championship

2000
Giants rout the Minnesota Vikings in the NFC title game to reach Super Bowl XXXV (the Baltimore Ravens win that game)

1970   1980   1990   2000   2010

1982
Redskins win the Super Bowl for the first time, beating the Miami Dolphins in game XVII

1986
Giants win their first Super Bowl by downing the Denver Broncos in game XXI

1987
Washington beats the Broncos in Super Bowl XXII

1992
Cowboys begin stretch of three Super Bowl victories in a four-season span

1991
Redskins win their third Super Bowl under coach Joe Gibbs, beating Buffalo in game XXVI

1990
Giants beat Buffalo Bills in Super Bowl XXV

STAT STUFF

TEAM RECORDS (THROUGH 2007)

Team	All-time Record	Number of Titles (Most Recent)	Number of Times in Playoffs	Top Coach (Wins)
Dallas	446–326–6	5 (1995)	29	Tom Landry (270)
New York Giants	626–529–33	7 (2007)	29	Steve Owen (153)
Philadelphia	496–541–25	3 (1960)	20	Andy Reid (96)
Washington	552–503–27	5 (1991)	22	Joe Gibbs (171)

NFC EAST CAREER LEADERS (THROUGH 2007)

Category	Name (Years With Team)	Total
Dallas		
Rushing yards	Emmitt Smith (1990–2002)	17,162
Passing yards	Troy Aikman (1989–2000)	32,942
Touchdown passes	Troy Aikman (1989–2000)	165
Receptions	Michael Irvin (1988–1999)	750
Touchdowns	Emmitt Smith (1990–2002)	164
Scoring	Emmitt Smith (1990–2002)	986
New York Giants		
Rushing yards	Tiki Barber (1997–2006)	10,449
Passing yards	Phil Simms (1979–1993)	33,462
Touchdown passes	Phil Simms (1979–1993)	199
Receptions	Amani Toomer (1996–2007)	620
Touchdowns	Frank Gifford (1977–1986)	78
Scoring	Pete Gogolak (1966–1974)	646
Philadelphia		
Rushing yards	Wilbert Montgomery (1977–1984)	6,538
Passing yards	Ron Jaworski (1977–1986)	26,963
Touchdown passes	Ron Jaworski (1977–1986)	175
Receptions	Harold Carmichael (1971–1983)	589
Touchdowns	Harold Carmichael (1971–1983)	79
Scoring	David Akers (1999–2007)	897
Washington		
Rushing yards	John Riggins (1976–79, 1981–85)	7,472
Passing yards	Joe Theismann (1974–1985)	25,206
Touchdown passes	Sammy Baugh (1937–1952)	187
Receptions	Art Monk (1980–1993)	888
Touchdowns	Charley Taylor (1964–1977)	90
Scoring	Mark Moseley (1974–1986)	1,206

MEMBERS OF THE PRO FOOTBALL HALL OF FAME

Player	Position	Date Inducted
Dallas		
Herb Adderley	Cornerback	1980
Troy Aikman	Quarterback	2006
Lance Alworth	Flanker	1978
Mike Ditka	Tight End	1988
Tony Dorsett	Running Back	1994
Forrest Gregg	Tackle/Guard	1977
Michael Irvin	Wide Receiver	2007
Tom Landry	Coach	1990
Bill Lilly	Defensive Tackle	1980
Tommy McDonald	Wide Receiver	1998
Mel Renfro	Cornerback/Safety	1996
Texas E. "Tex" Schramm	President/General Manager	1991
Jackie Smith	Tight End	1994
Roger Staubach	Quarterback	1985
Randy White	Defensive Tackle	1994
Rayfield Wright	Tackle	2006
New York Giants		
Morris "Red" Badgro	End	1981
Roosevelt Brown	Tackle	1975
Harry Carson	Linebacker	2006
Larry Csonka	Fullback	1987
Ray Flaherty	Coach	1976
Benny Friedman	Quarterback	2005
Frank Gifford	Halfback/Flanker	1977
Joe Guyon	Halfback	1966
Mel Hein	Center	1963
Wilbur "Pete" Henry	Tackle	1963
Arnie Herber	Quarterback	1966
Robert "Cal" Hubbard	Tackle	1963
Sam Huff	Linebacker	1982
Alphonse "Tuffy" Leemans	Halfback/Fullback	1978
Tim Mara	Owner	1963
Wellington Mara	Owner	1997
Don Maynard	Wide Receiver	1987
Hugh McElhenny	Halfback	1970
Steve Owen	Coach/Tackle	1966
Andy Robustelli	Defensive End	1971
Ken Strong	Halfback	1967
Fran Tarkenton	Quarterback	1986
Lawrence Taylor	Linebacker	1999
Jim Thorpe	Halfback	1963
Y. A. Tittle	Quarterback	1971
Emlen Tunnell	Defensive Back	1967
Arnie Weinmeister	Defensive Tackle	1984

MORE STAT STUFF

MEMBERS OF THE PRO FOOTBALL HALL OF FAME

Player	Position	Date Inducted
Philadelphia		
Chuck Bednarik	Center/Linebacker	1967
Bert Bell	Owner/Commissioner	1963
Bob "Boomer" Brown	Tackle	2004
Mike Ditka	Tight End	1988
Bill Hewitt	End	1971
Sonny Jurgensen	Quarterback	1983
James Lofton	Wide Receiver	2003
Ollie Matson	Halfback	1972
Tommy McDonald	Wide Receiver	1998
Art Monk	Wide Receiver	2008
Earle "Greasy" Neale	Coach	1969
Pete Pihos	End	1970
Jim Ringo	Center	1981
Norm Van Brocklin	Quarterback	1971
Steve Van Buren	Halfback	1965
Reggie White	Defensive End	2006
Alex Wojciechowicz	Center/Linebacker	1968
Washington		
George Allen	Coach	2002
Cliff Battles	Halfback	1968
Sammy Baugh	Quarterback	1963
Bill Dudley	Halfback	1966
Albert Glen "Turk" Edwards	Tackle	1969
Ray Flaherty	Coach	1976
Joe Gibbs	Coach	1996
Darrell Green	Cornerback	2008
Ken Houston	Safety	1986
Sam Huff	Linebacker	1982
David "Deacon" Jones	Defensive End	1980
Stan Jones	Guard/Defensive Tackle	1991
Sonny Jurgensen	Quarterback	1983
Paul Krause	Safety	1998
Earl "Curly" Lambeau	Coach	1963
Vince Lombardi	Coach	1971
George Preston Marshall	Owner	1963
Wayne Millner	End	1968
Bobby Mitchell	Wide Receiver/Running Back	1983
Art Monk	Wide Receiver	2008
John Riggins	Running Back	1992
Charley Taylor	Wide Receiver	1984

GLOSSARY

annually—each year

commissioner—the person in charge of a sports league

consecutive—in a row

consistent—performing the same or close to the same over a period of time

contract—an agreement to do something (in this case, play football for a team)

core—an important group

draft—held each April, this is when NFL teams choose college players to join their teams; teams with the worst records the prior year choose first, but draft picks can be traded to move a team's draft order

flamboyant—bold, or showy

franchises—more than just the teams, they are the entire organizations that are members of a professional sports league

media—reporters from television, radio, newspapers, magazines, and the Internet

New Deal policy—a program started by President Franklin Delano Roosevelt in the 1930s to help the United States recover from the Great Depression

overtime—a period of play after the regular time

playoffs—after the regular schedule, these are the games played to determine the champion

postseason—the period in which the playoffs are held

professional—someone who is paid to perform an activity (in this case, play football)

ratified—voted in favor of

retractable—can be opened or closed

rivalries—people (or teams) who compete for the same goal

rookie—an athlete in his or her first season as a professional

scrambling—when a quarterback runs, whether to buy time to find a receiver or to run downfield to gain yards

Super Bowl—the NFL's annual championship game, played in late January or early February at a different stadium each year

thrived—prospered

FIND OUT MORE

Books

Goodman, Michael E. *The History of the New York Giants.* Mankato, Minn.: Creative Education, 2004.

Schmalzbauer, Adam. *The History of the Philadelphia Eagles.* Mankato, Minn.: Creative Education, 2004.

Stewart, Mark. *The Dallas Cowboys.* Chicago: Norwood House Press, 2006.

Stewart, Mark. *The Washington Redskins.* Chicago: Norwood House Press, 2007.

On the Web

Visit our Web site for lots of links about the NFC East: *http://www.childsworld.com/links*

Note to Parents, Teachers, and Librarians: We routinely verify our Web links to make sure they are safe, active sites—so encourage your readers to check them out!

INDEX

Aikman, Troy, 10, 11
Allen, George, 31

Barber, Tiki, 18
Battles, Cliff, 28
Baugh, Sammy "Slingin' Sammy", 27, 29–30, 31
Bednarik, Chuck "Concrete Charley", 22
Bell, Bert, 21
Bergey, Bill, 23
Bledsoe, Drew, 11
Brandt, Gil, 8
Brown, Jerome, 24
Burress, Plaxico, 18, 19

Carmichael, Harold, 23
Conerly, Charlie, 14, 16
Cunningham, Randall, 24

Dietz, William "Lone Star", 28

Fassel, Jim, 18

Gibbs, Joe, 27, 30, 31, 33
Gifford, Frank, 16
Grange, Red, 15

Hein, Mel, 13
Howell, Jim Lee, 16
Huff, Sam, 16

Irvin, Michael, 10, 11

Jaworski, Ron, 23
Johnson, Jimmy, 10
Jones, Ed "Too Tall", 9
Jones, Jerry, 10
Jurgensen, Sonny, 31

Landry, Tom, 6, 7–8, 9, 10, 16
Leemans, Tuffy, 13
Lewis, D. D., 11
Lilly, Bob "Mr. Cowboy", 8
Lombardi, Vince, 16

Manning, Eli, 18
Manning, Peyton, 18
Mara, Jack, 18
Mara, Tim, 13–15, 18
Mara, Wellington, 18
Marshall, George Preston, 27, 28, 30
McNabb, Donovan, 20, 24, 25, 26
Mitchell, Bobby, 31
Montgomery, Wilbert, 24
Murchison, Clint, Jr., 7

Neale, Earle "Greasy", 21

Owen, Steve, 13, 15, 16
Owens, Terrell, 11, 12, 24, 25

Parcells, Bill, 11, 12, 17, 18
Phillips, Wade, 12
Pihos, Pete, 21
Portis, Clinton, 32, 33

Reid, Andy, 20, 25, 26
Riggins, John, 33
Romo, Tony, 11, 12
Ryan, Buddy, 24

Schramm, Tex, 7, 8
Simms, Phil, 15
Smith, Emmitt, 10, 11
Snyder, Daniel, 33
Spurrier, Steve, 33
Staubach, Roger "Captain Comeback"; "Roger the Dodger", 8, 9
Stewart, Tony, 33
Strahan, Michael, 18

Taylor, Charley, 31
Taylor, Jim, 22
Taylor, Lawrence, 17–18
Tittle, Y. A., 16
Tunnell, Emlen, 16

Van Brocklin, Norm, 22
Van Buren, Steve, 20, 21, 22
Vermeil, Dick, 23

Westbrook, Brian, 26
White, Reggie, 24

Zorn, Jim, 33